BEFORE YOU REALLY GET INTO THIS BOOK, TAKE A FEW MINUTES OUT TO LEARN SOME VERY IMPORTANT—

SPORTS DAFFYNITIONS

UMPIRE:
A GUY WHO CALLS MORE STRIKES THAN A UNION LEADER.

BASEBALL:
NINE GUYS IN SEARCH OF A TV SPONSOR.

FOOTBALL:
A CLEAN SPORT BECAUSE IT HAS SCRUB TEAMS.

BASKETBALL:
FIVE PLAYERS WHO NEED HANDKERCHIEFS BECAUSE THEY'RE ALWAYS DRIBBLING.

PRO BASKETBALL:
FIVE PLAYERS AND AN ACCOUNTANT.

PRIZE FIGHTER:
A GUY WHO IF HE DOESN'T HAVE A GOOD RIGHT IS LEFT.

3

SWIMMING INSTRUCTOR:
A HOLD-UP MAN.

QUARTERBACK:
THE ONLY GUY ON THE TEAM WHO KNOWS HOW TO COUNT.

A TENNIS PRO:
A PLAYER WHO IS SATISFIED WITH NET PROFITS.

A BAD HOCKEY PLAYER:
A GUY WHO SMELLS ON ICE.

A WRESTLER:
A GUY WHO DOESN'T WANT TO GET A HOLD ON HIMSELF.

CHESS:
A GAME THAT IS ALWAYS PLAYED ON THE SQUARE.

PRO ATHLETE:
A PLAYER WHO GETS PAID ABOVE THE TABLE.

WACKY

SPORTS

by TONY TALLARICO

THIS BOOK IS DEDICATED TO-
   MAN OF WAR, PELE, TED WILLIAMS,
   PEEWEE REESE, CARL FURILLO, KYLE
   ROTE, JR., MUHAMMAD ALI, JOE LOUIS,
   GEORGE PLIMPTON, TERRY BRADSHAW,
   LYNN SWANN, TONY DORSETT, THURMAN
   MUNSON, JOE DiMAGGIO, PETE ROSE,
   DAVE PARKER, MARIO ANDRETTI, STEVE
   CAUTHEN, TOM WATSON, NANCY LOPEZ,
   JACK NICKLAUS, CHRIS EVERT, BRAD
   PARK, PREACHER ROE, GORDIE HOWE,
   ROGER STAUBACH, JIMMY CONNORS,
   GEORGIO CHINAGLIA, PETE MARAVICH,
   JULIUS ERVING, BILLY COX, ROBERTO
   CLEMENTI, WILLIS REED, TY COBB,
   MICKEY MANTLE, LEW ALCINDOR, ANDY
   VARIPAPA, GLENN DAVIS, DOC BLANCHARD,
   BRONKO NAGURSKI, BEN HOGAN, BILL
   TILDEN, BOBBY RIGGS, JESSE OWENS,
   AND MOST OF ALL TO **YOU**!

ISBN 0-590-31588-9

Copyright © 1980 by Tony Tallarico. All rights reserved. Published by Scholastic
Book Services, a Division of Scholastic Magazines, Inc.

12 11 10 9 8 7 6 5 4 3 2   10   0 1 2 3 4 5/8

WEIGHT LIFTER:
A GUY WHO CAN PICK UP 5,000 POUNDS, BUT CAN'T PICK UP A CHECK IN A RESTAURANT.

GOLF:
A GOOD WALK IN THE OUT-DOORS RUINED.

PESSIMIST:
AN OPTIMIST ON HIS WAY HOME FROM THE RACE TRACK.

GREAT CADDY:
A PERSON WHO DOESN'T KNOW HOW TO COUNT YET.

A TIGHT END:
A FOOTBALL PLAYER WHO IS CHEAP.

HOCKEY:
A BOXING MATCH ON ICE BETWEEN TWO TEAMS.

LACROSSE:
GAME PLAYED BY PEOPLE IN THE RACQUETS.

HALL OF NO FAME

JOHN T. KIRKWOOD

JOHN THOMAS KIRKWOOD,
Pitcher, San Francisco, N.L. 1968
Never played. He took his $200,000 bonus money and moved to Paris, France.

MILTON "BIG MOUTH" WAINWRIGHT,
Pitcher, Boston, N.L. 1934-1945

Only pitcher to be sent to the showers while still in the locker room. In 1936, he hit 21 batters in one game. He claimed he had on someone else's glasses. Voted in 1941 player most likely to go into the armed forces on the other side. In 1943 he struck out 24 batters in one game but still lost it 56 to 3. Took bets on 1947 World Series. In 1940 he swallowed resin bag by mistake. Thought it was a potato knish.

ORLANDO JUAN ZUCKERMAN,
Left Fielder, Salt Lake City, N.L. 1805-1828
Benched 43 times in June for forgetting his name. First outfielder to say: "I lost the ball in the sun." Holds record for eating 24 hotdogs in one game. Never took a sign or a shower. Hit 7 doubles in one game. Also drank that many after game. In 1935 he drowned in a carwash.

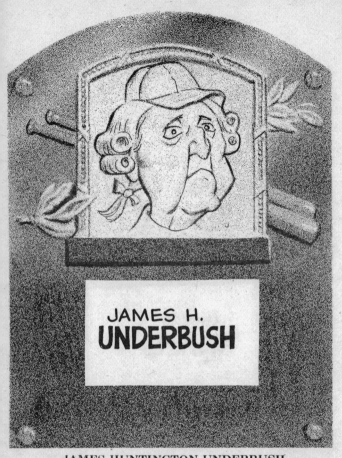

JAMES H. UNDERBUSH

JAMES HUNTINGTON UNDERBUSH,
Manager, East Orange, N.J. A.L. 1795-1803
Won pennants in 1766, 1775 and 1902. In 1784 he came in third which wasn't easy since there were only two teams in the league at that time. He is credited with inventing the double play, bunt, steal, catchers glove, home plate and the radio. Was first player to wear number on back of uniform. His number was ¼. After retiring from baseball in 1903, he opened up a chain of empty tents.

TIMOTHY K. KREEL

TIMOTHY K. KREEL,
Pitcher, New York, N.L. 1935-1937
Holds record for falling asleep on mound 24 times in 1936. Threw a 34-hitter in 1937. Wore glove on right hand and left foot. In 1935 he won 0 and lost 37 games. Blamed it all on his hangnail. Only major league pitcher to wear his uniform inside-out.

EDWARD "PEPPER" FRIMP,
Center Fielder, Philadelphia, N.L. 1912-1923
Voted player most likely to take a drink in 1912-1923.
Caught a fly ball in 1915. Got a hit in 1917. Fell off a bar
stool in 1912-1923. Never wore sun glasses but he did
own a seeing eye dog. Benched by his manager in 1919
for having bad case of dandruff. Kicked out of baseball
in 1923 for taking bets on turtle races.

ARNOLD "IGGY" QUIGGS

ARNOLD "IGGY" QUIGGS,
Catcher, Chicago, A.L. 1924-1928
Set record in 1925 when he bumped into the dugout water cooler 7 times in 9 games. Only player to throw umpire out of game. Ended career by being hit in the mouth by wife. First catcher to wear shin guards and after-shave cologne. Never met Babe Ruth or Jack The Ripper.

JOSEPH THEODORE NELSON BEAMISH,
Shortstop, Cleveland, A.L. 1903-1965

Batted .408 in 1904 but it didn't count. Umpires discovered he was using bat made out of cement. Voted player nicest to his mother 5 years in a row. Holds record for getting lost in every American league city. Never played in an All-Star game, but once saw one on TV.

13

HOWARD L.
ZILCH

HOWARD LLOYD ZILCH,
Third Base, Boston, A.L. 1902-1926
Never got into a game, but his uniform did fit him. In
1922 he was sent up to pinch hit but the game was rained
out. In 1914 his mother did not let him play entire
season. She had sent him to his room without his
dinner and just forgot about him for 277 days. In 1924
he got mugged. In 1916 he got married to a waitress
whose first name was Gladys.

CLARK "CATFISH" VOODOO,
Right Fielder, Cincinnati, N.L. 1932-1939

Set record in 1935 for running into right field wall 58 times in a double header on an odd numbered day. Notorious for having bad breath. Beaned 4 times in one game in 1937. Always wore spats on and off the field. Never hit a homer, but he does know how to spell it. Banned from baseball in 1939 for setting fire to the town of Pittsburgh.

FORD "DIRTY SHIRT" VANDERBILT,
First Base, Brooklyn, N.L. 1925-1929
Caught a cold in 1927. Played three games in 1928.
Picked up a bat and four girls in 1929. In 1926 he got a
haircut. In 1925 he learned how to tie his shoes and
open his locker. Ended his career in 1929 by being gored
by a mad bull in the bullpen. Once shook hands with
Lou Gehrig.

CHARLES R.
ZAMP

CHARLES ROCKWELL ZAMP,
Second Base, Detroit, A.L. 1899-1905
Compiled a lifetime batting average of .784. Hit 983
homers, stole 23,000 bases and two airplanes. In one
game he hit 6 homers while standing on his head. In the
same game he handled 53 chances and made 52 errors.
In the sixth inning he went into the stands and sold 529
hotdogs and 325 score cards. In 1905 he retired from
baseball to open up a drive-in dentist office. 17

BASEBALL TIP...

HOW TO STEAL SECOND BASE

① ② ③

FOOTBALL TIP...

THE TACKLE

① ② ③

21

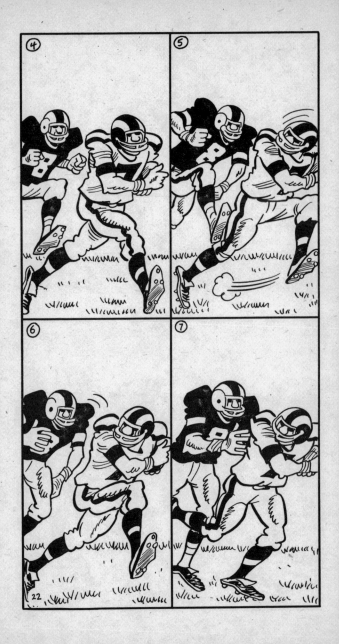

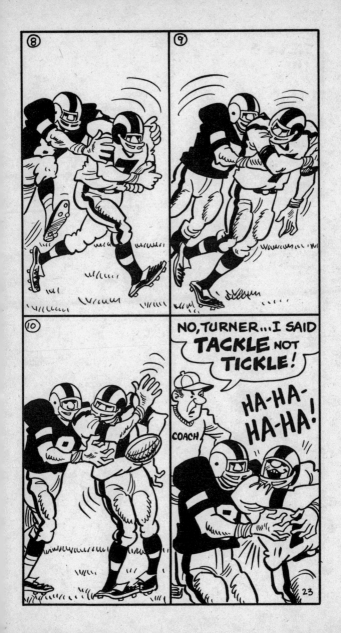

TENNIS
TIP...

THE SERVE

①

②

③

OLYMPIC HOCKEY

28

29

EVERYTHING YOU ALWAYS WANTED
TO KNOW ABOUT *FOOTBALL*...
BUT DIDN'T KNOW WHO TO ASK *!!*
AND YOU STILL WON'T AFTER YOU'VE READ THIS.

THE GAME ALWAYS
STARTS OFF WITH
A KICK-OFF.

THE FOOTBALL IS RECEIVED AND THEN CARRIED UNTIL THE PLAYER IS STOPPED.

BEFORE THE SNAP, A HUDDLE IS CALLED BY THE OFFENSE AND STRATEGIES ARE DISCUSSED.

A PLAY IS THEN GIVEN.

THE DEFENSE TRIES EVERYTHING TO STOP THE OPPOSING TEAM.

THERE ARE TWO BASIC PLAYS USED TO MOVE THE BALL.

THE QUARTERBACK'S JOB IS TO PASS THE BALL.

IF A PASS IS INTERCEPTED, THE OFFENSE CAN ELECT TO PUNT.

TO WIN, A TEAM MUST SCORE A GOAL.

TO PREVENT SCORING, LINESMEN
BUILD A DEFENSIVE WALL.

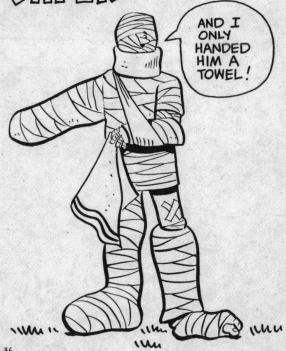

LOONY

GUIDE TO...
MAKING FOOTBALL SAFER (FOR YOURSELF)

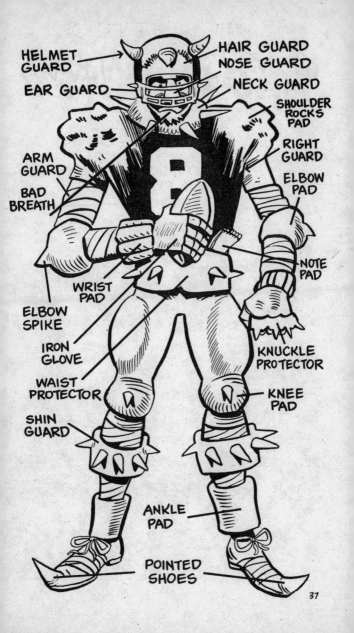

SPORTS FOTO-FUNNIES

THEY CALL THIS A RACE TRACK? SO FAR I'VE BEEN PULLED OVER BY THE POLICE FOUR TIMES FOR SPEEDING!!

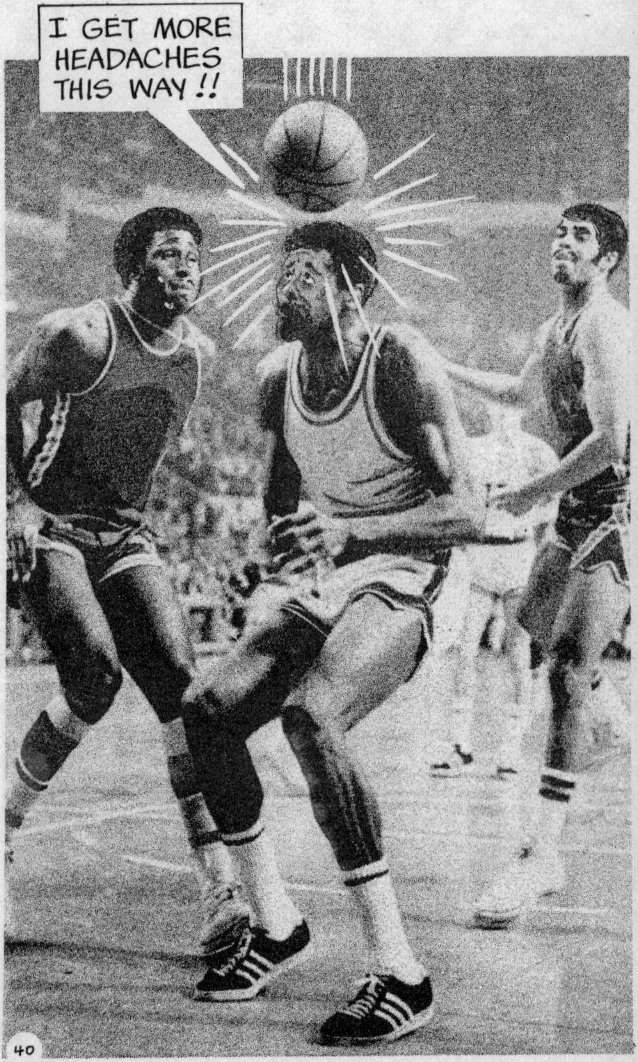
I GET MORE HEADACHES THIS WAY!!

THE ACTION GAME OF

SOCKER!!

SPORTS QUIZ

SCORING: 10 POINTS FOR EACH CORRECT ANSWER.
20 POINTS FOR EACH INCORRECT ANSWER.
THE PERSON WITH NO SCORE AT ALL IS THE WINNER!

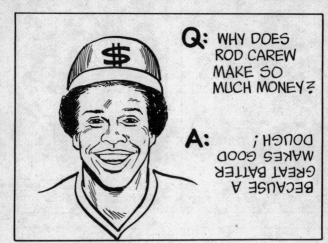

Q: WHY DOES ROD CAREW MAKE SO MUCH MONEY?

A: BECAUSE A GREAT BATTER MAKES GOOD DOUGH!

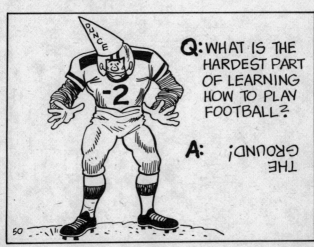

Q: WHAT IS THE HARDEST PART OF LEARNING HOW TO PLAY FOOTBALL?

A: THE GROUND!

Q: WHY SHOULD A SWIMMER NEVER GO INTO THE WATER AFTER A MEAL?

A: BECAUSE HE WON'T FIND ONE THERE!

Q: WHY SHOULD A BOWLING ALLEY BE QUIET?

A: BECAUSE YOU WANT TO HEAR A PIN DROP!

FOR LOSERS

SKIING

CANOEING

BOXING

VOLLEYBALL

WEIGHTLIFTING

SHOOTING

FENCING

BASKETBALL

JUDO

SOCCER

SPEED SKATING

POLE VAULT

CYCLING

GYMNASTICS

BELIEVE IT...

IRVING ORR OF THE BOSTON BUMBERS, WORE THE SAME PAIR OF ICE SKATES FOR 10 YEARS THOUGH HIS WIFE DIVORCED HIM FOR SHREDDING THE BED, SHEETS AND RUG.

ORR NOT!

HOOLEY ORR OF THE KANSAS CITY CANS, ONCE BROKE BOTH HIS ARMS. (NOT IN A GAME BUT IN JOE'S BAR AND GRILL) HE ALSO HAD A WEIGHT PROBLEM. EVERYTHING HE ATE WENT TO HIS WALLET.

GOALIE **BABE ORR**, OF THE WORLD-FAMOUS OHIO ROCKHEADS, NEVER ATE WHALEBLUBBER, BUT HE DID TRY A PEANUT BUTTER AND SHOE POLISH SANDWICH. HE DIDN'T LIKE IT! HE CLAIMED THE PEANUT BUTTER MADE HIS TONGUE STICK TO THE ROOF OF HIS MOUTH.

TIM ORR OF THE TORONTO CHICKENS, PERFORMED THE HAT TRICK 18 TIMES IN ONE MONTH ....

HOWIE

THE IMMORTAL **HOWIE ORR**, OF THE N.Y. WRANGLERS, *NEVER* SUFFERED AN INJURY IN THE 15 YEARS HE WAS ON THE TEAM. MAINLY BECAUSE HE NEVER PLAYED A SINGLE GAME!

...HE WOULD PULL A RABBIT OUT OF IT EVERY-TIME THINGS GOT DULL ON THE ICE.

USING SPORTS
PERSONALITIES IN
COMMERCIALS AND
ON PRODUCTS HAS
PROVED SO SUCCESSFUL
THAT WE URGE OTHERS
TO FOLLOW IN THEIR FOOT
STEPS!!

REDDIE!
OR NOT

IN THE NEXT
FEW PAGES ARE
SOME THINGS WE
WANT YOU TO RUSH
TO YOUR FAVORITE
STORE AND ASK FOR!
(PLEASE DON'T TELL THEM
WE SENT YOU!)

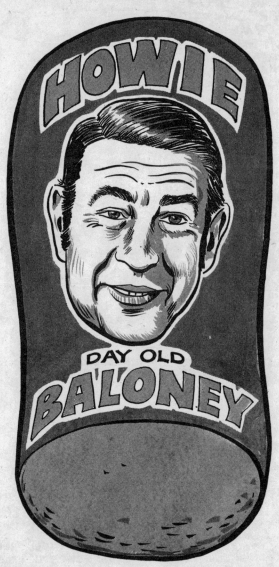

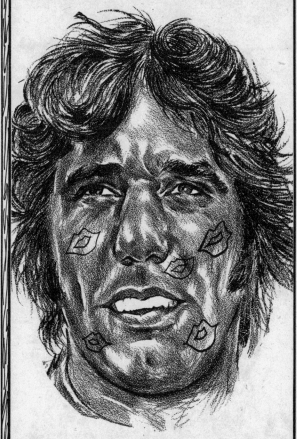

JOE NAMATH

FAMOUS FOR HIS GREAT PASSES

DATING SERVICE

65

UNOFFICIAL BASKETBALL

GOAL IS GOOD OR GOSH I NEED A MANICURE.

HOLDING AN OPPONENT OR I GOT NO PULSE.

ILLEGAL USE OF HANDS OR ONE GUY GAVE ANOTHER PLAYER A KARATE-CHOP.

ILLEGAL DRIBBLE OR I GOT A NEW YO-YO AT HOME.

SIGNALS

CHARGING OR PUSHING OR NO AUTOGRAPHS.

STOP CLOCK FOR A FOUL OR NO IT'S THIS HAND THAT HAS THE M AND M'S.

TRAVELING WITH BALL OR SPEED UP THE GAME, I'M DOUBLE-PARKED.

TIME OUT OR HERE COMES ANOTHER COMMERCIAL.

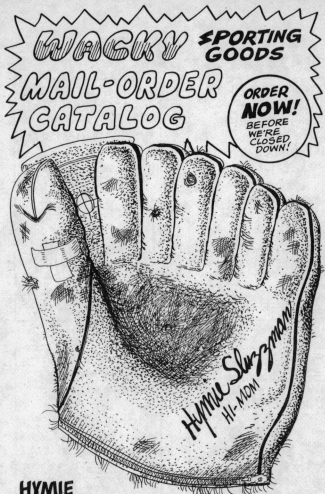

HYMIE SLUZZMAN AUTOGRAPHED FIELDERS GLOVE

MADE OF DURABLE CHICKEN FAT AND YAK WOOL. PRE-GREASED WITH 99% SARDINE OIL. NEVER USE GLOVE IN WARM WEATHER. HYMIE LEARNED TO WRITE HIS NAME ESPECIALLY FOR THIS. **$347⁸⁹** AS IS

TIP-TOP GRAIN DUCKHIDE
COVER MAKES THIS ALMOST

PRO SOCCER BALL

ONE OF THE FASTEST SELLERS
ON THE MARKET. HAS SOME
STITCHING BUT IS MOSTLY
STAPLED TOGETHER. OFFICIAL
SIZE IF YOU HAPPEN TO BE
PLAYING IN LILLIPUT. COLOR:
BLACK AND GANGRENE GREEN.

$ 7 ⁵³
$9 ⁰⁰ INFLATED

9 POWER, 987 MM

BINOCULARS

WITH A FIELD OF VISION OF
ABOUT 18". GREAT FOR WATCHING
FOOTBALL, BASEBALL, HORSE
RACING OR STREAKERS.
SIMULATED CARDBOARD
CARRYING CASE WITH STICKY
BACKING.

$ 32 ⁹⁹   WITHOUT LENS **$ 1 ⁵⁰**

89-INCH STRAIGHT

HOCKEY STICK

WITH A COUPLE OF CURVES.
PEANUT BUTTER FILLED
HANDLE. PLACE FOR
NOTCHES WHEN YOU
HIT SOMEONE OVER
THE HEAD.

SHIPPING
WT. 65 LBS.

$ 14 ⁰⁰

WITH PRE-CUT NOTCHES—

$ 29 ⁰⁰

NURF'S TOP-GRAIN IMITATION PLASTIC **FOOTBALL**. THE OFFICIAL *BUSTED TOES, N.J. LITTLE LEAGUE BALL!* HOLDS ITS SHAPE UNDER ANY CONDITIONS EXCEPT RAIN OR SNOW. RUGGED-FILLED WITH SOUR CREAM. BALANCED AERODYNAMICALLY EVEN THOUGH IT WEIGHS 64 POUNDS. TRY A FAST KICK—YOU'LL NEVER FORGET IT.

PRICED RIGHT AT ONLY $1.00 PER POUND

NO POWER IMPACT—NO PRO

FOOTBALL HELMET. GLASS TRIPLE-LAYERED FOR THICKNESS ACROSS FOREHEAD, BACK, EARS, NOSE AND THROAT. ADJUSTABLE ROPE CHIN STRAP, FITS HEAD SIZES 6½ TO 24 ¾.

$2.00

$18.49

WITH BUILT-IN WIPERS

HERE YOU ARE FANS, OVER-
RIPE —JUICY—

TOMATOES.

WONDERFUL FOR THROWING
AT BASEBALL, FOOTBALL
AND BASKETBALL PLAYERS.
U.S. GOVERNMENT INSPECTED.
3 IN A CARTON.
GUARANTEED TO SPLASH
ON CONTACT!

3 FOR **54¢**
65¢
WITH SEEDS

FAMOUS MAKER (*IRVING FAMOUS*)

TENNIS
RACKET

STRINGS FROM
CONTENTED CATS.
SANDPAPER
HANDLE,

$43⁰⁰

FOR THOSE WHO
ARE IN THE RACKETS,
18¢

FAMOUS ATHLETES

WHERE ARE THEY NOW?

MELVIN "CRAZY-NOSE" FLUMP

THIS FORMER STAR FULLBACK FOR THE OLD CHICAGO CHICKENS LIVES IN MOLEHOLE, TEXAS AND RUNS A USED TURTLES SHOP. HE IS 87 YEARS OLD AND FALLS DOWN A LOT. HE ENJOYS WATCHING FOOTBALL ON TV AND STILL PRACTICES TIEING HIS OWN SHOES!

WALT
"THE JERK"
KLUNK

SUPER-STAR CENTER OF THE LEGENDARY ROCK ISLAND PICK-POCKETS. IN ONE GAME WALT SCORED 93 BASKETS AND SOLD 370 CANS OF SODA. HE NOW RESIDES IN HAIR-CUT, KENTUCKY AND SELLS FORGED VAN GOGH PAINTINGS!

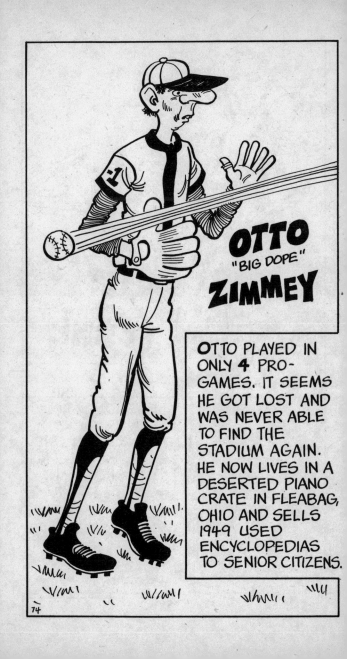

OTTO
"BIG DOPE"
ZIMMEY

OTTO PLAYED IN ONLY **4** PRO-GAMES. IT SEEMS HE GOT LOST AND WAS NEVER ABLE TO FIND THE STADIUM AGAIN. HE NOW LIVES IN A DESERTED PIANO CRATE IN FLEABAG, OHIO AND SELLS 1949 USED ENCYCLOPEDIAS TO SENIOR CITIZENS.

74

MICKEY
"YELLOW BACK"
QUIGGY

MICKEY HAD 196 FIGHTS AND WON **2** OF THEM. HE HOLDS THE RECORD FOR BEING THE ONLY BOXER TO BE KNOCKED OUT IN THE DRESSING ROOM, BEFORE THE FIGHT. HE CALLS A PARKING LOT IN BRRRR, ALASKA HOME AND MAKES THINGS OUT OF BLUBBER.

THE 3 GREATEST SPORTS INTERVIEWS OF ALL TIME (ALMOST)

HERE AT THE WINTER OLYMPICS, WE HAVE JUST SEEN A GOLD MEDAL PERFORMANCE. TELL ME, WHAT GAVE YOU THE GREATEST DIFFICULTY IN YOUR EXHIBITION?

INTERVIEW #1

76

INTERVIEW #3

80

A LOOK AT...
LACROSSE

A LOOK AT...
SURFING

OLDE TIME
•SPORTS•

FOLKS PAY TO SEE A HORSE RACE, BUT HORSES ARE SMARTER! THEY NEVER PAY TO SEE THE HUMAN RACE!

DO SOMETHING DIFFERENT! FOOL HIM! TRICK HIM! HIT HIM!!

THERE IS SO MUCH WATER ON HIS BALL THAT WHEN A BATTER GOES UP TO HIT, HE CARRIES A BAT IN ONE HAND AND AN UMBRELLA IN THE OTHER. IN FACT THERE IS SO MUCH DEW ON THE BALL THAT A PLAYER ONCE HIT ONE INTO THE STANDS AND THREE FANS DROWNED!

THE LAST TIME I MADE THIS SHOT, MY PANTS FELL OFF!

89

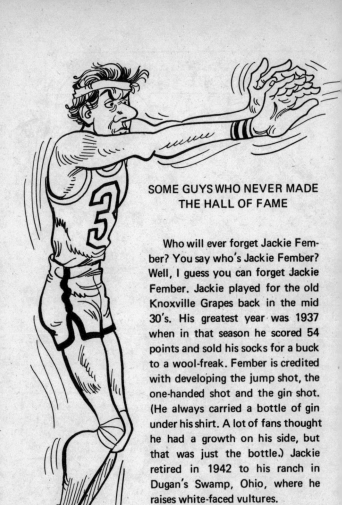

SOME GUYS WHO NEVER MADE THE HALL OF FAME

Who will ever forget Jackie Fember? You say who's Jackie Fember? Well, I guess you can forget Jackie Fember. Jackie played for the old Knoxville Grapes back in the mid 30's. His greatest year was 1937 when in that season he scored 54 points and sold his socks for a buck to a wool-freak. Fember is credited with developing the jump shot, the one-handed shot and the gin shot. (He always carried a bottle of gin under his shirt. A lot of fans thought he had a growth on his side, but that was just the bottle.) Jackie retired in 1942 to his ranch in Dugan's Swamp, Ohio, where he raises white-faced vultures.

When basketball fans get together to talk shop the name that's sure to pop up is the remarkable Artie "Soupy" Hoggstown. "Soupy" played the game for 83 years and called it fini at the ripe old age of 124. Hoggstown performed for such teams as the New York Nothings,

the Boston Baked Beans, the North Korean Giants, the Dallas Money-counters, the Buffalo Hitch-hikers and the Green Bay Nudists. "Soupy" once scored 97 points, then the other team showed up. He was famous for his fast dribble and chicken potpie. When he hung up his sneakers back in 1947, his last team, the Quebec Quilts retired his number and his recipe for chicken potpie.

Come on gang, let's hear it for Ford Bermer, the Galloping Gardenia. Ford played one game for the St. Louis Lox and walked off the court never to return. Ford said he didn't like the other guys.

Roy Underwoodson (Old Number 7529) played his ball for the Walnut Street Clowns. Roy was only 9 years old when he quit. One day he took his ball and went home. 64 years later he came out to buy a loaf of rye bread.

Kenny Yumm never played basketball but he did once see it on TV. His uncle, Rex Arnette, once knew a guy who lived three houses down from Nat Holman's house.

DID YOU HEAR ABOUT...

...THE DOPE WHO FLOODED THE GYM BECAUSE HIS COACH TOLD HIM TO GO IN AS A **SUB**!

...THE FIGURE SKATER WHO WAS SO GOOD SHE MADE THE FIGURE 8 THE HARD WAY — TWO **4**s !

...THE MOST POPULAR SPORT AT PRISONS IS **POLE VAULTING** !

ABZ'S WILD WORLD OF SPORTS IS PROUD TO BRING YOU THE **TRANSYLVANIA ALL STARS**!

CY CYCLOPS HAS BEEN BY FAR THE MOST THRILLING CENTER FIELDER IN THE HISTORY OF BASEBALL. IN ONE GAME THIS YEAR HE HIT 4 HOMERUNS, CAUGHT 20 FLYS, STOLE 10 BASES AND BURIED 3 UMPIRES. CY HAS A MEAN STREAK IN HIM BUT WRITES NICE POEMS.

FRANKIE HUNCHBACK'S IN LEFT FIELD, CAN REALLY CATCH FLYBALLS (MOST IN HIS TEETH). HAS A DRINKING PROBLEM AND HIS MANAGER WANTS HIM TO STRAIGHTEN OUT IN TIME FOR THE WORLD SERIES.

95

THE MUMMY IS OUR PICK FOR FIRST BASE. A REAL OLD TIMER, BUT STILL CAN GO GET 'EM ESPECIALLY VICTIMS. DOESN'T WEAR UNIFORM. JUST 60 YARDS OF BANDAGES.

CATCHER. THE GREAT, MICKEY FELM. STARTING HIS 193rd YEAR BEHIND THE PLATE FOR THE TRANSYLVANIA GLUGGS. USES A LIVE COUGAR FOR A GLOVE.

WOLFMAN IS AT THIRD BASE FOR THE 10th TIME IN 11 SEASONS (ONE YEAR HE WAS LOCKED UP IN A DOG POUND). PLAYS HIS BEST BALL WHEN THE STANDS ARE PACKED AND THERE'S A FULL MOON.

100

PETE PHANTOM IS OUR CHOICE FOR RIGHT FIELD. BATS RIGHT, THROWS LEFT AND KILLS WITH BOTH.

FRANKENSTEIN MONSTER, RIGHT HAND PITCHER—HASN'T HAD A BALL CALLED ON HIM IN 132 GAMES (WHAT UMPIRE WOULD BE DUMB ENOUGH TO CALL ONE WHEN HE'S PITCHING?) BEST PITCH: BLOODBALL.

"CATFISH" GLOOB, LEFT HANDED PITCHER. IN ONE YEAR HE STRUCK OUT 750 BATTERS DUE TO THE FACT HE HAS 4 LEFT HANDS AND THROWS 4 BALLS AT ONCE. BEST PITCH: FANGBALL.

THE DESIGNATED HITTER IS THE MIGHTY MICKEY SCREAMS. SO FAR THIS YEAR, MICKEY HAS A BATTING AVERAGE OF .937. HE HAS SLOWED DOWN A LITTLE, BUT HE STILL CAN GET FROM HOME PLATE TO HIS TOMB IN 9 SECONDS.

COLLECTING CARDS HAS ALWAYS BEEN A FAN'S DELIGHT. NOW, FROM THE BOTTOM OF AN OLD TRUNK, WE BRING YOU... **CRAZY** SPORTS CARDS

JIM "SKULL"
BONKER
OAKLAND CLAMS

ONCE TOSSED A PASS BUT THE GIRL SLAPPED HIS FACE.

Z06 JIM "SKULL" BONKER
WGT: 88 POUNDS SOAKING WET.
HGT: 10'3". DRY WGT: 44 LBS. OR 120 POUNDS. HOME: IN AN OLD JUKE BOX. HOBBY: SHARPENING BALL-POINT PENS.

MAJOR AND COLLEGE LEAGUE RECORD		
YEAR	TEAM	PASSES
1972	BOY SCOUT BULLDOGS	956,397
1973	(DID NOT PLAY - LOST IN PHONE BOOTH)	
1974	OAKLAND CLAMS	5 (IN A DICE GAME)
1975	(WILL NOT PLAY - GONE TO THE MOON)	

MILT "THE BUILT."
BRANNIGANO
TULSA THINGS

MILT ONCE TOSSED A
BASKETBALL AND A REF
INTO THE STANDS.

138 MILT "THE BUILT" BRANNIGANO
HGT: 145" WITH SHOES ON,
WGT: 3,673 TONS. HOME: LOCAL
POLICE STATION. HOBBY: READIN' THE
TELEPHONE BOOK.

CAREER PRO RECORD					
YEAR	TEAM	G.	F.G.	F.T.	PTS.
1970-71	KING KONGS	200	200	200	1
1971-72	ZOO PARADE	47	6	31	5,000
1972-73	TULSA THINGS	8	11	21	4
1973-74	TULSA THINGS	44	71	16	7½

MILT "DIZZY"
BEAMISH
CHICAGO PUBS

 OL' MILT WAS SENT TO THE SHOWERS SO OFTEN HE BECAME WATER LOGGED.

(936) MILTON "DIZZY" BEAMISH
HGT: 4'3". WGT: 307. FEET: 2.
THROWS: RIGHT UP. BATS: IN HIS
HEAD. BORN: 5-11-14, BROKEN GAS,
TEXAS. HOME: SOMETIMES.

MAJOR AND MINOR LEAGUE RECORD

YEAR	TEAM	G.	W.	L.	E.R.A.
1969	LITTLE LEAGUE				
1970	KNOXVILLE	5	2	8	ALOT
1971	PUBS	127	0	90	P-U
1972	(WAS OUT OF THE SEASON- DRUNK!)	25¼	0	HIS CAP	9.07
1973	PUBS				
1974	PUBS	57	1	56	MUCHO
1975	(FREE AGENT- DRAFT BEER)	0	0	77	88.06

BILLY "ELBOWS"
FLINKER
DETROIT
DING-BATS

BILLY ONCE ATE A BASKETBALL.... FOR DESSERT HE ATE SNEAKERS.

(107) BILLY "ELBOWS" FLINKER
HGT: 9'6". WGT. 807 ¾ LBS.
SCHOOL: COLLEGE OF WESTERN SHOP-
LIFTERS. BORN: 1964. HOME: IS WHERE
THE HEART IS. HOBBY: DIVING OFF
TALL BUILDINGS.

CAREER PRO RECORD				
YEAR TEAM	G.	F.G.	F.T.	PTS.
1970-71 NEW YORK FREAKS	80	0	1	1
'71-'72 CHICAGO CUPCAKES	(DIDN'T PLAY- HURT HIS HAIR)			
'72-'73 DETROIT PITS	107	2369	0	149,678
'73-74 PITTSBURG PIZZAS	3	0	5	2
	(WITH SAUSAGE TO GO)			

OMAR JUAN JEAN IVAN
GOMEZ
MOSCOW KNIGHTS

OMAR ONCE FELL OUT OF A
PLANE OVER LOS ANGELES
AND BROKE HIS SOCKS.

900,716 OMAR JUAN JEAN IVAN GOMEZ
HGT: 3' 1½". ANKLES: BROKEN
WGT: 9 STONES, 1 ON EACH HAND. HAT
SIZE: 17⅞, HOME: SUPERMARKET
SHOPPING CART, HOBBY: BUSTING TV'S.

MAJOR AND MINOR LEAGUE RECORD					
YEAR	TEAM	G.P.	G.	A.	PTS.
1834	APPOMATTOX	17	32	37	?
1901	ROMANIA	479	65	176	5
1915	BERLIN	3	47	14	144
1643	PUERTO RICO	31	0	0	⅓
39 BC	ROME	IX	VII	IX	XVII
1974	MOSCOW KNIGHTS	174	231	180	1

STEVE "BOOM-BOOM"
FERM
BOSTON
RED SNEAKERS

STEVE MADE 28 ERRORS IN ONE INNING WHILE SITTING ON THE BENCH

2½ STEVE "BOOM-BOOM" FERM
HGT: 5'8". WGT: 190. EARS: ON BOTH SIDES OF HIS FACE. THROWS: GREAT PARTIES. BATS: STANDING ON HEAD. BORN: EBBETS FIELD. HOME: A BROKEN-DOWN RICK-SHAW, TRANSYLVANIA, CALIFORNIA.

MAJOR AND MINOR LEAGUE RECORD
TOP SECRET

(IT'S REALLY VERY, VERY BAD, FANS)

Q: WHY DID GEORGE WASHINGTON CALL HIS SOCKS, "GOLF SOCKS"?

A: BECAUSE HE HAD A HOLE IN ONE!

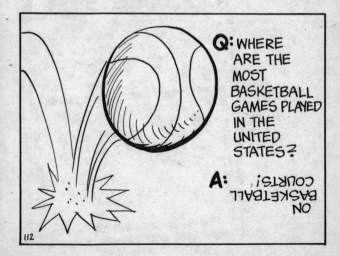

Q: WHERE ARE THE MOST BASKETBALL GAMES PLAYED IN THE UNITED STATES?

A: ON BASKETBALL COURTS!

Q: WOULD ABE LINCOLN HAVE TROUBLE GETTING A COLLEGE EDUCATION TODAY?

A: No! BEING AS TALL AS HE WAS, HE COULD EASILY GET A BASKET-BALL SCHOLARSHIP!

Q: WHAT DID THE SOCCER BALL SING TO THE PLAYER?

A: "I GET A KICK OUT OF YOU!"

BOWLING

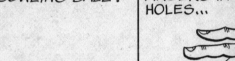

THIS IS A *BOWLING BALL!*  1	NOW PUT THREE FINGERS IN THE HOLES...  2

RRRIP

A SPLIT!

CLINIC...

A SPARE!

A STRIKE!

NO! NO! **NO!** NO BOUNCE TO THE OUNCE

CRASH

BALL MUST BE RELEASED!

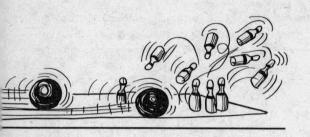

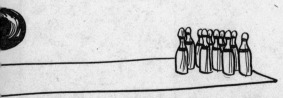

GUIDE TO U.J.O.'s
(UNIDENTIFIED JOGGING OBJECTS)

FIRST TIME JOGGER

BIG CITY JOGGER

LUNCH TIME JOGGER

ORIGINAL JOGGER

BACK TO WORK JOGGER

DIE-HARD JOGGER

SALES DAY JOGGER

LAST TIME JOGGER

BASEBALL

THEN   NOW

THE BAT

DON'T BREAK THAT BAT! IT'S THE ONLY ONE WE'VE GOT AND EIGHT OTHER GUYS HAVE TO USE IT!

HMM... MAYBE THE POLKA-DOT ONE THIS TIME... THE COLORS MATCH MY EYES FOR TV!

THE FIELD

I'M SO GLAD THE OWNER LET US USE THIS EMPTY LOT FOR TODAY'S GAME!

THIS NEW STADIUM EVEN HAS HEATED ASTRO-TURF!

BASKETBALL

THEN NOW

FINAL SCORES

THIS SURE WAS A HIGH-SCORING GAME. YOU DON'T SEE MANY 15-9 SCORES!

...HERE AT THE END OF THE FIRST PERIOD IT'S THE REDSKULLS 103 AND THE DRIBBLERS 97!

PAY

HERE'S YOUR EIGHT DOLLARS FOR PLAYING THIS MONTH AND DON'T FORGET IT'S YOUR TURN TO BUY THE BALL FOR THE NEXT GAME!

OK, WE'LL MEET YOUR TERMS... A MILLION FIVE PER SEASON, HALF INTEREST IN THE TEAM, A PRIVATE 747, A BURGER FRANCHISE BUSINESS AND 2 QUARTS OF MY BLOOD!

MAYBE?

HOCKEY

THEN

NOW

ATTENDANCE

LET'S SEE, COUNTING THE VENDERS AND THE ORGAN PLAYER, THERE ARE 23 PEOPLE HERE!

FANS ARE STILL LINED UP OUTSIDE FOR THIS GAME, WHERE THEY'LL PUT THEM I DON'T KNOW! THERE ARE ALREADY 91,000 HERE!

EQUIPMENT

I KNOW IT'S NOT MUCH, BUT IT'S MORE PROTECTION THAN NOTHING!

NOW, WHICH MASK SHOULD I WEAR?

FOOTBALL

THEN **NOW**

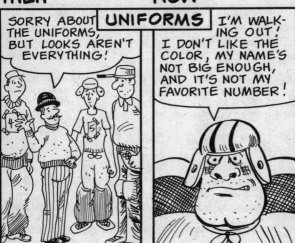

UNIFORMS

SORRY ABOUT THE UNIFORMS, BUT LOOKS AREN'T EVERYTHING!

I'M WALKING OUT! I DON'T LIKE THE COLOR, MY NAME'S NOT BIG ENOUGH, AND IT'S NOT MY FAVORITE NUMBER!

PLAYERS

JOE PLAYS DEFENSIVE TACKLE TODAY 'CAUSE HE WEIGHS THE MOST, 103 POUNDS!

OK, YOU'RE GONNA THROW THE PASSES TODAY, SKINNY!

ON THE BENCH..

ON THE BENCH..

DO NOT FEED THE PLAYER.

R PITCHER
DOING GREAT!
ONLY GAVE
23 HITS IN
E FIRST
NING!

THAT GUY CAN REALLY PITCH! HE GOT THE BALL OVER THE PLATE ON ONLY THREE BOUNCES!

KICK ME!

ITH THE OAKDALE ICERS!

D LIKE TO
TIRE BUT
JUST BOUGHT
NEW PAIR OF
OXING GLOVES!

I WON'T SAY HE'S DUMB, BUT WHEN HE WON HIS VARSITY LETTER, SOME ONE HAD TO READ IT TO HIM!

ZZZZZ

ON THE BENCH..

ON THE BENCH..

...RE IN EIGHTH ...CE, WHICH ISN'T ...SY TO DO SINCE ...RE ARE ONLY ...VE TEAMS IN ...IS LEAGUE!

A BIG CROWD FOR THIS TEAM IS WHEN TWO VENDERS AND AN USHER SHOW UP!

...S TEAM IS ...TERRIBLE ...AT ANY GUY ...O MAKES A ...SKET GETS ...STANDING ...VATION!

WE CAN'T GET A REFEREE SO WE GIVE EVERYONE WHO COMES TO THE GAME A WHISTLE!

LAST INTERVIEW!

HERE WE ARE AT THE SCENE OF THE MOST BOMBASTIC FLIGHT OF COURAGEOUS VALOR IN ALL OF AMATEUR SPORTS... THE GRUELING DOWN-HILL SKI EVENT! AND HERE WITH ME IS THE WORLD CHAMPION TO ANSWER THIS INSIGHTFUL QUESTION: *WHAT IS SECOND IN DIFFICULTY TO THE DOWNHILL RACE?*

THE UPHILL RACE!